Abe

1. hope you might
find this interesting

:)

Hugs

lou

the gift

a breakthrough in self transformation

ian lawton

Rational Spirituality Press **RSP**

First published in 2013 by Rational Spirituality Press.
All enquiries to be directed to www.rspress.org.

A CIP catalogue record for this title is available from the
British Library.

ISBN 978-0-9572573-5-1

Cover design by Ian Lawton.
Cover photograph by Lilkar, licensed by dreamstime.com.
Author photograph by Gaia Giakali.

Printed and bound by Henry Ling Limited, Dorchester,
England.

the three timeless
treasures of transformation

If we're going to take this journey together, I'll have to ask you to put yourself in my shoes. So summon your imagination and picture this...

You're a big-shot consultant and project manager in the commercial world, earning big money. Nice cars, nice women, nice holidays, nice houses, nice life. But increasingly you've been feeling this isn't who you really are, that your life is a sham. You feel suffocated, trapped, desperate. Then suddenly something happens – it may only be small, but it's the straw that breaks the camel's back – and you just know you've got to get out. It's now or never. So you quit.

You become interested in alternative things: Egypt's pyramids, Atlantis, reincarnation, the spiritual path. You become an author, even though you never consciously planned it.

For once you believe in what you're doing, but your books don't catch on well enough to provide even a basic income. So you sell your house, and from the profits you buy a boat to live on. Then you're forced to sell your boat and just live off the

1

money. It doesn't last long but you're happy because you're where you're meant to be.

After several hard years you get a break. Just when you thought you could never go back to the commercial world, an opportunity arises for you to use your old skills to train other people in how to manage projects. For a few years you're more or less square with the bank, and you even get to live in a nice rented flat by the sea. You can work part time and still write and research. Fantastic! You even train as a regression therapist to add another string to your bow.

But suddenly the company who provide you with training work goes bang, without warning. They're one of the big players and now there's a glut of experienced trainers on the market. Most of them have more contacts than you and your work dries up, not helped by a worsening economy.

One friend kindly puts you up in their flat rent free for a year. But you can't outstay your welcome so you borrow the money from another dear friend to convert a big old Mercedes van into a mobile home to live in. He and his lovely partner even let you live in it on their drive for eighteen months. But you can't see clients in a van, and anyway you're living in the middle of nowhere.

You've carried on believing passionately in your spiritual work. After all you've come up with several new, thought-provoking concepts such as Rational Spirituality and the holographic soul. In the past people regularly wrote to tell you how much your work had helped them, sometimes even that you're a brilliant researcher.

So you've carried on battling against the odds, and by now you've written more than ten books covering a wide range of topics in every conceivable way – complex research-based books, simple pocket ones, novels. Yet overall sales have steadily decreased, and in the last few months they've dwindled to almost nothing. People hardly even talk to each other about your work any more, let alone to you.

You've been meditating every day for years, envisaging every positive outcome conceivable, chanting manifestation mantras. Your therapy training meant you had to clear many emotional blockages, and even since then you've had close colleagues – the best therapists around – checking you for any that remain. All to no avail.

Somehow it seems like most of your friends have deserted you too. You contact them but usually they don't even respond. You've thought about ending it all plenty of times recently, lying alone on your bed in your cramped living space, sometimes beating your head with your fists in frustration.

One day you look in the mirror and are startled to see bruises all over your forehead. Yellow and purple reminders of your inner turmoil.

One thing has kept you going throughout this most painful period. Your deep love for a woman, and her deep love for you. She's married with children, it's complicated, and not without its own pain. You plan a future together, after a long and painful process she and her husband separate, then they're forced back together by love of their children – anything to take away their pain. You

4

try to have no contact but the love is too strong. She still feels the same but can offer you no hope.

Yet you cling to it. After all, it's all you have.

Then suddenly, the final bombshell. So totally unexpected that you've never even remotely contemplated it. She's fallen massively for someone else. Love at first sight. The real deal. Her bond with him is even stronger than the one she shared with you, and she simply cannot resist.

There's no deliberate intent to hurt you, but in an instant you're an afterthought, a mere footnote to the new things in her life. You have no idea if she'll be able to achieve the lifelong happiness with him that she never could with you. But it doesn't matter anyway, because you don't matter any more.

You've had a chequered love life. You've broken plenty of hearts yourself, but recently you've been on the receiving end. Too many times. You can't go through this again, not when it's worse than ever before because you love her so much. Not, too, when she was the one lifeline you had left.

You were already right on the precipice, and now you feel it crumbling under your feet. You're in an agony of doubt and rejection and above all fear... always the fear.

So what the hell do you do?

You discover THE GIFT...

I don't even begin to claim that I've completed my spiritual journey in the physical plane, or even that I'm in any way more 'spiritual' or 'advanced' than anyone else. Such ideas have always been, and remain, a complete anathema to me.

Indeed I'm well aware that my journey continues and that anything I have to say now is merely a reflection of my current state of awareness and experience. It will almost certainly evolve in time. Yet I do feel strongly that my recent transformative experience has been hugely empowering, and that it may as yet be a relatively rare or at least significant one.

In my case it was initiated by having a broken heart. This is pretty much guaranteed to affect all of us at least once in each lifetime, and in the modern world maybe more. So if sharing my experience helps even one person to respond to the same situation by using THE GIFT to transform themselves, it will have been worth it. Yet I have a strong sense that it can be brought to bear in other situations that involve intense pain too.

In order to put THE GIFT into context, some time back the idea of 'timeless treasures of transformation' came through to me. I sensed that as a result I should try to define a list of the key goals, in terms of transformation of consciousness, that have been consistently pursued by all souls who've ever incarnated in modern human form on our planet. The very challenges that, once mastered, allow us to move on from the reincarnation cycle. Initially I'd intended to build one of my novels around them and had scratched around trying to work out what they were, but I didn't feel massively confident in the list of ten I ended up with when I broke off.

Yet when THE GIFT presented itself and I knew I had to write about it, it was immediately clear this was where the treasures should first be revealed. Not least because it's an integral part of one of them. What's more my complex and ill-defined list of ten effortlessly morphed before my very eyes as I began to draft the outline, each slotting under one of just three umbrellas: the treasure of *inner peace*, the treasure of *conscious creation* and the treasure of *being love*. Even then they overlap and interact hugely, but some degree of differentiation helps us to focus.

THE GIFT is the most challenging aspect of the third treasure. What is it? In short it involves nothing less than facing our *very worst* fears head on *as they arise* and *transmuting* them into love *there and then*. So it's more than just choosing love over fear in every situation, which is the more commonly discussed aspect of the treasure of being love. As far as I'm aware this kind of active transmutation of our worst fears is rarely even mentioned as a theoretical idea, let alone described as a practical experience. It is seriously challenging stuff.

By contrast the *main* aspects of *all* three treasures are all well known and widely practiced in the modern world. Indeed innumerable self-help and other books have covered the three topics, and their authors have done a brilliant job in helping huge numbers of people to wake up and get to a certain point. So, apart from THE GIFT itself, what else can I hope to bring to the party?

Well, I have a strong sense that, especially to those in real pain and difficulty, many of these books can feel somewhat remote – perhaps even as if they're making things out to be very simple when, for some of us at least, they quite clearly aren't. And that can make us feel inadequate, as if somehow we're less deserving than those authors who've learned how to manifest everything they want and to live a wonderful, abundant life. I'm not for one moment suggesting they haven't, or that the example they've set hasn't inspired people in their tens of thousands. Yet, for some of us at least, while the *theory* might be simple, putting it into *practice* can be quite another matter.

So I feel strongly that many of you are ready for something different, perhaps with a slightly harder, though still loving, edge. I guess I'm here to talk about what happens when the going gets really tough. About what happens when, for whatever reason, you *don't* benefit from a sudden, wonderful, one-off transformation or even ascension, after which everything is abundance and bliss – as incredible as that must be. About what happens when, instead, you take two steps forward then one step back. About those times when you have to really struggle to fight your way through the dense jungle the spiritual path sometimes throws up.

And sometimes it *is* a fight, and you need all your courage to overcome your challenges. This is where I'll be bringing the wonderful concept of the spiritual *warrior* into play.

Of course the use of my own experiences means I've opened up some of the most intimate aspects of myself and my life, and I did briefly wonder if I couldn't present them as general illustrations or anonymous case studies. But the three timeless treasures are themselves so entirely concerned with truth, integrity of intent and love that to do so would have somehow cheapened this whole endeavor.

Although to follow the spiritual path truly and with total honesty and love is *not* easy, and requires consistent dedication and effort, I know from experience that it does become easier with practice. The major transformative steps we take along the way are difficult but hugely rewarding. They're all designed to help us reach the point where we fully reflect our true spiritual selves while still in human form. What's more, in the end they *do* lead to a level of consciousness in the physical that truly is a state of total abundance and grace, where everything just flows from a wellspring of pure love.

This is what we're all striving for, what we're all here to achieve. Having said that we can choose to go at whatever pace we want. Some are more focused on the prize while others are happier to just enjoy the journey, but we should always remember this isn't a race, there are no prizes for 'growing faster' than someone else, and we get as many lives as we like to get it right.

Especially as far as THE GIFT itself is concerned,

you can't just try to bring it straight into your life anyway. You'll have to wait for the next time a major personal challenge of the right sort strikes. But when it does I hope you may be ready to take that huge step in the transformation of your consciousness.

Because this is deliberately only a short, easily digestible book I've been inclined to concentrate on what I see as the most important aspects of each treasure, and also to assume a certain amount of general prior knowledge of spiritual topics. Three of these stand out and need to be emphasized:

☞ The physical world is merely a reflection of infinitely complex and dynamic interactions taking place on an energetic, nonphysical level. Because of this the reality you experience in the physical is formed from your beliefs, intentions, thoughts and words. Learning to direct these consciously rather than unconsciously is the second treasure, but for now the crucial point is the implication:

you have complete and total responsibility for creating the life you experience; down to the tiniest detail; with no exceptions. This is so fundamental as to be a non-negotiable aspect of any informed spiritual worldview.

☞ Although we're all part of the 'One', or the universal consciousness of 'Source', or whatever you choose to call it, there's strong evidence that we're *also* individual consciousnesses or souls who lead many lives in order to *experience* being wealthy and poor, feted and ignored, loved and spurned, strong and weak, clever and stupid, and everything in between. This simultaneous oneness and individuality is expressed in my concept of the 'holographic soul'.

☞ Although it's by no means certain that you had a *detailed* 'life plan' before you came into this one, you may have at least planned for certain major probabilities to be on your path to help you face specific and well-devised challenges that aid your spiritual growth. Yet, rather than this involving any sort of predestiny, your free will to make your own choices and divert from your path is paramount. All this should only serve to reinforce your sense of personal responsibility, not detract from it.

Details of further background reading that can fill in any gaps in these and other areas are provided at the end.

the treasure of

inner peace

The treasure of inner peace acts as an umbrella for a number of key elements of the spiritual warrior's toolkit.

inner voices & meditation

We must learn to hear and listen to our inner voice whenever it speaks to us, whether by a strong intuitive feeling about a place or person, or an unusual synchronicity or even series thereof, or by any other means it chooses. These and other triggers may well be intended to keep us on our chosen life path. It doesn't matter whether we see these as the promptings of our own higher self, or of a spirit guide, or of anything else we care to choose. All this helps us to learn to come from the heart rather than the head when it's appropriate. To see how we *feel* about any decision we have to make, rather than what we *think* about the different options open to us.

Nothing does more to enhance our ability to connect with our inner voice, and to foster spiritual growth generally, than a daily meditation routine. What's more, because it's *effort* and consistency *of intent* that matters most, this holds true pretty much irrespective of its duration and content. So you routine may include mantras, affirmations and visualization when your focus is on conscious creation, and in their own right these give the less experienced something to focus on. But if you're more experienced and your focus is on enhancement of consciousness generally, you may prefer to empty your mind completely. This is far harder but brings its own rewards with time and perseverance.

self love

A very good indication of how well we love ourselves can be gained by looking at how we love others, and in particular how we love our partners. The experienced warrior will know all about how the vast majority of people who don't know any better project their own inadequacies onto a partner who doesn't appear to suffer from them, expecting said partner to complete them in those very areas where they themselves feel incomplete. Both parties are likely to be doing this based on different inadequacies, and both will tend to become increasingly unhappy once the initial honeymoon period is over because they're expecting the impossible.

In its worst form the person feels they're incomplete without a partner, end of story. Their whole life is a search for fulfillment through the love of another, and when one relationship breaks down they hardly pause before rushing headlong and full of false hope into the next. Indeed such rebounding is the mechanism many people use to avoid having to face the pain of a broken heart, despite the common and well-founded advice about the dangers of such addictive behavior. Because endless rebounds are merely a recipe for increasing dis-ease.

Once we understand how this works all such relationships can clearly be seen to be based on *need* far more than on love. Yet I expect most of us have been fooled by this most common of illusions to varying degrees. I know I fell prey to it repeatedly in my earlier life.

Nevertheless the experienced warrior comes to realize that neither partner can *ever* make the other truly and lastingly happy if they're not happy *within themselves*. Only then can we ever be ready to love someone else in a healthy, non-needy way. Only then, provided we've listened to our instincts and chosen a partner who is in the same emotionally secure space, will two people truly manage to make the whole more than the sum of its parts.

dropping the mask

To achieve such a high measure of self love we have to know who we are in the first place. That means having the courage to drop the mask we all become accustomed to wearing for the outside world, and to go deep within and recognize those aspects of ourselves we often prefer to ignore. Some call them our 'darker side' or our 'lower self', but there's really nothing abnormal here at all. We all bring unperfected emotional traits into incarnation with us. They're the very things we're seeking to transform.

One person might be predominantly playing the victim and have a tendency towards self pity. Another might be controlling and a bully, but only as a reaction to other inadequacies. The 'game of human life' works in such a way that these emotional inadequacies are often deliberately reinforced in childhood, to ensure they're alive and kicking and ripe for transformation in our adult life – but only if we're prepared to own and face them first.

There are many ways to achieve this. Regression therapy, for example, may uncover patterns repeating across past lives and into this one. But in the modern world there exist a wide variety of therapeutic techniques that help us to reach inside and transform those things that might otherwise cause serious dis-ease if left unaddressed. Some may seek the help of a hypnotherapist or counselor, others may use self-help books or just meditation and their own intuitive techniques to do whatever needs to be done.

The important thing here is there are no hard and fast rules. What works for one won't necessarily work for another. Some people bring less emotional 'baggage' into this life to be dealt with than others, either because they're having a rest or perhaps because they've worked through most of it in other lives and are now ready to reap the full rewards. In either case they probably won't need any sort of therapy or even a great deal of introspection. Indeed for them achieving inner peace may not even mean very much, because it's something they've always had and they don't even notice it.

It's also worth remembering there can be many 'layers to the onion'. So you can think you've uncovered everything that needs to be exposed, only to find there's more baggage lurking further inside. This is frustrating but must be accepted. You can try and take a rest between layers, but often your higher self will seem to have other ideas. In the next section I'll recount my own experience of not recognizing the fundamental inner part of me that most needed to be faced.

Above all, I'd strongly urge you not to let anyone *else* tell you where you're at or what you need. Use your own intuition. If you feel dissatisfied with your life and seem unable to improve it despite your best efforts, you may want to change your approach, and you might even consider enlisting some help. On the other hand, if you're happy with your life, feel entirely comfortable in your own skin and don't sense you've ever really been hiding any aspect of yourself, you're probably just fine as you are.

happiness from within

One way you'll know if you're at least well on the way to a healthy level of self love will be when your happiness comes almost entirely from within rather than without. But this too is by no means easy.

From the time we're born we're totally dependant

on the love and support of our parents – our mother in particular – which psychologically conditions us to look outside for our happiness and wellbeing. As we grow this search for external wish-fulfillment is transferred onto material things: if only we had *that* toy we'd be happy. We badger and we pester and if we're lucky enough to have compliant parents with money our wish is granted. But what happens next? Within hours, days tops, we're onto the next thing.

Most people aren't so different as adults. As spiritual warriors we can't resist a slight smile when we see how people stuck deep in the material illusion still think that if only they had *that* hairdo, *that* car, *that* dress, *that* holiday, *that* pair of shoes, *that* house, or worst of all *that* partner... *then* they'd be properly happy. But each time they fulfill a desire another one comes along to take its place, usually one that's just that little bit more demanding.

That's why it should come as absolutely no surprise when the pampered children of the wealthy commit suicide in deep depression, or overdose on drugs. They didn't even have the fulfillment of having to work hard to chase the material illusion.

being not striving

Probably *the* most important aspect of inner peace is to recognize that *striving* after happiness will almost never result in the real thing. Because we'll always be chasing something that in one moment seems only just round the corner, and in another further off than ever. That's not to suggest that hard work, dedication and dreams have no place. They do. But if they're unbalanced and all-consuming they can lead to false expectations of fulfillment.

But look at professional sportspeople, you might say. If they didn't have that all-consuming focus they'd never be able to achieve what they do. This is absolutely true, and long may they carry on giving us such excitement and pleasure. But in fact the ones at the absolute pinnacle provide a supreme example of exactly what we're talking about.

They chase the buzz of winning *that* race, *that* game, *that* fight, *that* championship, *that* world medal, and so on and so forth. Yet what do they pretty much all describe when they achieve it? First of all it's a little dreamlike, they can't really believe they've finally done it. Then for the *very best* there's invariably a sense of anticlimax, even emptiness, to varying degrees. So they keep on going, chasing the next one, always wanting to be better, to feel that all-too-temporary buzz again. Within five minutes of a major win, those at the absolute top are already thinking about the next challenge.

What happens when finally their skills start to wane? The more balanced individuals get out and manage to realize the journey was far more important than the destination. They find other worthwhile outlets into which they can channel their drive, focus and determination. But others are not so balanced and spiral downhill.

So what should the spiritual warrior be doing instead? The trick is not to *do* anything, except turn our normal thinking on its head. As soon as we stop thinking that if we *do* this or *have* that we'll be happy and fulfilled, we allow ourselves to just stop and *be* happy. Right *here*, right *now*.

Whatever our circumstances, if right here, right now we have a roof over our head, we're healthy and free, and have food in our stomach, water to drink and air to breath, then we have all we need to be truly happy. We can climb to the top of a mountain, throw our arms out wide and give thanks. We can marvel at a bird soaring on high. Or we can stare in amazement at a snowflake. This kind of appreciation of the incredible wonders of the world we live in may sound clichéd, but it's no less true for that. These wonders are all around us all the time, but we're so used to taking them for granted they rarely receive our focus. Yet each and every natural wonder that surrounds us can act as a constant reminder that our life is a perfect gift just as it is, and that we need nothing else to just *be* happy.

At least that's the theory. It's a majestic one we should all attempt to put into practice, and sometimes it *does* feel easy to just *be* joy. But, as we'll see from my own example shortly, at other times it's very, very hard, and to pretend otherwise is surely counterproductive.

nonattachment & impermanence

Nonattachment is another aspect of inner peace that experienced spiritual warriors will have heard and read plenty about. Yet it's one of the hardest spiritual principles to nail down and put into any proper perspective.

It originates in the notion that, in order to escape the bonds of the addictive wheel of reincarnation, we should generate no more karma whether 'good' or 'bad'. I'd argue this gives it a false start in many different ways: not least because there's no such thing as good or bad, whether we're discussing karma or anything else; and because growth and experience, rather than unfathomable karmic laws, are the dynamic forces that underlie our many lives.

That aside I'd suggest there's still something of importance in this idea of nonattachment, it merely needs some qualification. For a start it surely can't mean we should be completely *devoid* of emotion when, one way or another, everything about our transformation involves love. This is why I prefer to talk about *loving* nonattachment.

What does this mean in practice? In one sense it's not loving *so* intensely that you're destroyed if the object of your love – a house, a career, a partner, even a child – is taken away by whatever means. What's more *if* the worst happens it means being able to react with love and gratitude for what you were fortunate enough to have, rather than with fear, anger or regret about what you've lost. To that extent it starts to bring in elements of the treasure of being love, as we'll see in due course.

As for the related concept of *impermanence*, a spiritual warrior learns to treat apparently good and bad news just the same, because lost in the folds of either may be the opposite just waiting to spring a surprise. So developing a deep sense of equanimity – that is, not celebrating one's apparent successes or good fortune too much, but not being unduly downhearted by apparent failures and bad fortune either – is clearly an important element of inner peace. Yet arguably this too is only a prelude to using the treasure of being love to reframe any apparent failure or bad fortune and turn it into its complete opposite.

One other thing all the greatest sources of spiritual wisdom are clear about is that turning to asceticism and isolation is not the true way to gain inner peace. Indeed it's easily achieved if you withdraw from the world and all its complexities, but you're hardly being tested under these circumstances. Most of you will have been away on a meditation or other form of retreat, then come back into the real world to find all your best intentions of retaining that wonderful sense of serenity and love succumbing under the weight of everyday human challenges – of families, relationships and work.

That's when we're reminded that transformation is no walk in the park.

the six aspects model

My own particular experience of transforming consciousness by developing my sense of inner peace is I think an interesting and perhaps unusual one, and therefore it's hopefully worth sharing in some detail.

I expect like many of you, over a number of years I gradually came to realize that material things no longer made me happy – to such an extent I now genuinely feel I want for nothing, even though I live in a van and have relatively few possessions that haven't been given away to friends or to charity. One exception is when I was trying to find a rare part for one of the two classic motorbikes I've rebuilt in recent years, but the enjoyment there was much less in the owning and more in the creative process of restoring and redesigning.

This realization began to dawn more and more after I moved to Dorset around four-and-a-half years ago to live by the sea, and found myself increasingly drawn to taking long walks in its incredible countryside. Unlike material things, I found these completely transformed me. Repeatedly I'd find myself standing on a high ridge with panoramic views for miles around, or on a cliff overlooking the sea, just throwing my arms in the air and shouting THANKYOU!! to anyone in the nonphysical who might be listening in.

I even began to collect driftwood from local beaches and to create mirrors and other unusual pieces of artwork. Both the collecting and the creation filled me with a deep inner joy.

What's wonderful is that, for a time at least, the less I had the more grateful I was. When all this started in earnest I'd just come out of a serious relationship and for the first time ever I spent more than a year with no partner, no dates, nothing. I was living alone and didn't even have that much of a social life. I loved it. At last my joy really was coming from within.

But as I suggested earlier there are limits, and I

feel that since that time I've explored them pretty thoroughly.

To understand this, let's use a simple model of human life that contains six key aspects: our work, within which is subsumed our main finances; our hobby, if this is not the same; our health; our partner and children, if we have them; our other family; and our friends.

Now, to the extent that nonattachment is about being able to let go without too much suffering, we can probably cope with significant loss in just one of these six areas *relatively* easily. Maybe even two. So, for example, you lose your job and your best friend dies, both within a short space of time. This is hard, especially if you're not experienced at coping with loss. But if you're reasonably balanced you'll take huge comfort from the fact you still have, for example, your health, your spouse, your children, your family and your other friends. You'll learn to focus on the good not the bad, and to be thankful for what you *do* have rather than resentful over what you *don't*.

I'm not going to go through each stage one by one, because you'll already be getting the picture. The interesting thing about my own experience is that only a little while ago I *felt* I was down to just one-and-a-bit of the six aspects giving me any sort of comfort or purpose in life. Let me explain.

To expand on the scenario I presented at the outset, by this summer I'd been living in my van in a small village in north Dorset for more than a year. My lovely flat by the sea had gone two years before when the training work started to dry up, and ever since then the inner peace I'd felt so proud of achieving had been increasingly put to the test.

Now I found myself with virtually no commercial work and, with book sales plummeting too, no money of any consequence coming in. I have no children of my own, which in one sense is a blessing when you're in such a sorry state, but to counterbalance this I've seen them be a massive comfort, indeed a reason to live, to friends facing difficult times in their own lives. For some years

I'd also been distancing myself from my family, none of whom have ever had the slightest interest in the spiritual path. Meanwhile a series of events had led me to believe I'd lost *most* of my former friends, particularly in the regression community, although in hindsight this was only partially true.

What I did have left were first my health, although that was becoming questionable from a mental if not a physical perspective; and second my two closest friends, the wonderful couple who'd been kind enough to let me stay on their drive. They could see how hard I was battling to remain positive when everything around me was crumbling to dust, but I wasn't always successful, and even the closest of friends have their limits of patience.

One massive problem was that this was clearly no temporary difficulty, because the downward spiral had continued unabated for several years – and bear in mind the next section will reveal I'm only skimming the surface here. My experience was, quite objectively, that as one door shut another slammed in my face. So even expecting anything other than more bad news was becoming *extremely* hard.

What made all this worse was that I knew I had so much potential, in every area of my life. I was blessed with a good brain and health, a reasonable physique and so on. I'd had a privileged education. I'd been given all the opportunities anyone could ask for, and to make matters worse I knew what success was – in business, in sport when I used to race bikes and then cars, even with my earliest books. Yet this was where I'd got myself. On the inside I felt like a worthless nothing living in a van.

This was when the love I was still clinging to for dear life dropped the first real bombshell. Despite all our plans to create a new life together, and all the months of fighting through the slow process of persuading her husband it would be better for them to part, her children reacted so badly when this did finally happen that guilt consumed her. We'd already had little chance to see each other since we first fell in love, but instead of the situation improving it got worse. Yet I still didn't see it coming when, about four months into their separation, she told me she was taking her husband back.

The only thing that stopped this producing the total heartbreak I faced more recently was that I knew how much she still loved me. Yet I still had to come to terms with the fact they'd be sharing a bed again, and that if we had any sort of future together it was now not months but years away. For both of us the pain of not being able to be together was always fighting against the love we had to see which would win out, but we agreed we had to let each other go and, for a time at least, had no contact. It wasn't the first time, but it was still immensely sad for both of us.

Now my dark night of the soul really started to intensify.

I spent literally hundreds of hours lying on my bed staring at the ceiling, trying to work out what the hell it all meant. I went round and round in circles.

Sometimes I'd think I had it all worked out, then another thought would come on another day and I'd be more confused than ever. This was when my frustration grew so intense that I beat my forehead hard enough to bruise it.

One thing I clung to was that I'd let her go with genuine love, notwithstanding my own pain. I even managed to hope that she and her husband would find some sort of real happiness together. Lots of people talk a good game about how, if you love someone, you must let them go with love and move on. But perhaps they haven't tried it when the love is very strong and, more especially, the rest of their life is in tatters.

Of course at the time I didn't know this was just a practice run for what THE GIFT itself would give me in due course. But even at that time I did feel I was facing one of the hardest tests of loving nonattachment and of inner peace that could be faced. After all I'd already pretty much lost four of the key aspects of my life, and now I was losing a fifth and questioning the sixth.

What's really interesting is that, only about six months into our relationship, she had reluctantly made a strange revelation: 'I keep getting the same message. Again and again and again. You have to *lose everything*. Including me.' What we didn't know was that would only really happen much later.

All this partly feeds into further revelations in the next section to do with conscious creation, but hopefully it also shows just how hard *real* inner peace is to achieve. It's always worth remembering that it's easy enough when most of the six aspects of your life are going well or even just ok. But if you get to the point where you face serious challenges in the majority, say in three, four or more of them, holding onto your inner peace is really, really hard.

I guess the message is never to be complacent about inner peace, especially if yours hasn't been *properly* tested yet. Yet if you get to the point where you can retain it even when all the six aspects of your life are in disarray, I'd say there's a pretty good chance you've mastered everything the human experience has to offer.

the importance of hope

At this dark point I decided that maybe my challenge was to learn to live without any hope *at all*. Of *anything*. So I tried to live with a complete absence of expectations, desire or attachment. I tried to accept that I was almost completely isolated and that my life had no real purpose, and just to see where that led me.

This particular bit of my story does *not* have a happy ending. This truly *was* the darkest hour for my soul.

I look back on it now and still it makes me shudder. For about a week I became like a zombie. I can tell you now that the realm of no hope is not one I'd advise you to visit voluntarily. It's certainly not one I intend to go back to in this life, nor in any other if I can help it.

So I allowed myself to have hope again, for my

writing and research if nothing else. I came to the conclusion that we can exist without almost everything that normally gives us comfort in life, perhaps even love at least for a time, as long as at all times we feel *needed* in *some way* by *someone*. Whether it's as an employee or parent or sibling or lover or friend, as long as we feel *someone* needs us for *some purpose*, then we can survive. Almost certainly we won't be a balanced human being without rather more than just that, but to me this is the absolute minimum requirement for basic survival.

That is, of course, unless we've developed to the point where we *can* feel completely content without any sense of being needed or loved by anyone but ourselves. But again I'd suggest that anyone who's reached that point has fully mastered the human experience.

All this time another battle was raging in my head. Had my incarnate self really been subconsciously creating this quite incredible absence of abundance for more than two years? Or could I at least partly blame my higher self, and a life plan hell bent on pushing me to my limits?

At the time I could find no answer, but now I think I have it. I'll share it with you in the next section.

the treasure of

conscious

creation

The alternative word often used for this treasure is *manifestation*. But I prefer *conscious creation* because, as discussed at the outset, we manifest our physical experience via our beliefs, our intentions, our thoughts and our words. The important point is that we naturally do this from our subconscious – that is, *unconsciously*.

So this treasure is all about learning to *consciously* direct our experience of the physical world. It's about learning to proactively take control of it, instead of seeming to be always reacting to blind chance, fate or the terrible whims of some all-powerful deity.

Again there are a number of aspects to it, all of which interact.

the power of now

Your life, my life, everyone's life is a series of points in time. To be more accurate, everyone's experience of the physical is a series of 'now-moments'.

How can I say this with such certainty? Because we've built up more than enough scientific and channeled evidence that our human perception of moving *from* the past, *through* the present and *into* the future is merely something we've developed to allow us to make sense of the physical world. With so much information flooding our senses and so great a desire to analyze it all, our perception of time and the ability to file away apparently past events is what stops we humans from simply frying our brains.

From the perspective of creating our reality we need to understand that we do this in every now-moment. Yet we spend the vast majority of our waking hours not enjoying the moment at all, but looking backwards or forwards. Not only that but, especially when the treasure of inner peace is underdeveloped, we often insist on focusing on the less favorable aspects of our experience.

So if we're dwelling on a past problem we're allowing unfavorable thoughts to influence our reality *now*, when what we should be doing is learning from it if necessary, letting it go and then just enjoying the now. Or if we're worrying about a possible future event we're allowing unfavorable thoughts to influence our reality *now*, when what we should be doing is appreciating it's not a certainty, taking any actions we can now to produce a favorable outcome, letting it go and then just enjoying the now.

Either way by choosing to put our focus into something we regard as unfavorable we're giving it power in the now, and one way or another and to a greater or lesser extent it will influence one or more of our future now-moments.

Consider what you've been thinking since you started this section. Has your focus strayed at all? Have I triggered you to start thinking about unfavorable things in your so-called past or future just by writing about how we tend to dwell on them? In this particular case I'm not suggesting that's an unfavorable thing because hopefully you're either learning or reinforcing something very important. But we all know how easily we can allow our thoughts to wander off.

On the other hand, if your whole intent in reading this book is to further transform your consciousness, and you're giving it your full focus, and it's resonating with you, then the mere act of reading these words will be having a profound impact on you on an energetic level *right now*.

The true spiritual warrior maintains their full consciousness entirely in the now. Of course while they're training themselves it wanders off, but they catch it by making sure their 'observer self' is vigilant and simply *canceling* unwanted or unnecessary thoughts. Over time their thoughts will wander less and less. This is where meditation focused on emptying the mind can be so useful, but there are other techniques too, many developed in the Orient and involving martial arts and other exercises in focus and self discipline.

You've heard about sports people who are 'in the zone'. Sport is an obvious example but it applies equally to all areas of our lives, and we all achieve this state from time to time. You know, when everything is just effortless and flowing? Spiritual warriors have simply trained themselves to be *in* the zone far more often than not.

One thing I'd like to emphasize about the power of now is that it does *not* mean *all* thoughts are your enemies. Only *undirected* ones are.

the power of belief

There are myriad books describing different techniques for conscious creation and it would be pointless to attempt to describe them all here. Most are fairly consistent at heart, which is what we might expect given that we're actually talking about a basic understanding of how life works possessed by the wisest humans for thousands, if not tens of thousands, of years. So what I'd like to do here is focus on what I see as the most important aspects of conscious creation.

One area of significant dispute concerns how specific your affirmations and visualizations should be. My advice would be this. If you're trying to make major changes to one or more whole aspects of your life, almost to who you are as a person, then be as flexible as possible. If you concentrate on *what* you want and *why* you want it, rather than on exactly *how* and *when* you're going to get it, you're giving the underlying mechanisms of the universe the maximum scope to fulfill your desire.

By contrast if you're dealing with something very specific, like a favorable outcome to a one-off, make-or-break meeting, or on filling up spaces on a workshop, then the more detail you can put in the better. In that case don't just visualize, use *all* your senses – hearing, smell, even taste if it works for you. Go right into how the fulfillment of your desire *feels* for you and for any other people involved, because you're aiming for positive *feeling* at least as much as you are positive *thinking*. But be aware that being specific is harder, especially for the beginner and especially if the timescales are short.

Apart from that distinction nothing, absolutely nothing, is more important than your *belief:* first in the general fact that your reality is created by you and you alone, whether it's consciously or unconsciously; and second in your unlimited *power* to direct it exactly as *you choose*, especially if you combine your belief with *enthusiasm*.

It's often said that the sky's the limit with conscious creation, and there are indeed very few limitations. Admittedly it's probably true that if we're missing a limb we can't just regrow it by the power of belief alone. But some sources insist we can do other amazing things that would have major benefits for most of us.

One of my favorite suggestions, which has always resonated hugely, is that you can slow down the biological ageing process simply by not falling for the accepted scientific view that as you get older you become more infirm. Again there will be some limits but at the very least if you fully believe you're ten, even twenty years younger than your birth certificate says, and continue to believe that, arguably that's what you'll manifest. Indeed in later life what's to stop you upping the figure by ten years every decade? Time will then truly stand still...

We place our own limitations on the creation process purely through *lack* of belief. That's why it's as well to start small and build up. If you have any doubts at all about the intention you're trying to fulfill, the chances are it won't come to fruition. Having said that we all know of people who had what everyone else considered to be an impossible dream, who made it come true against all the odds purely by the force of their determination and belief. Let them be a shining example to you when you're ready.

To illustrate the power of belief, I'd be prepared to bet there's at least one favorable thing in your life that you've *always* believed in, so much so that you hardly give it a thought. It might be 'I never get ill' or 'I just know I'm going to live a long time'. If these are true, long-lasting intuitions and not just passing fancies, it almost certainly means they're challenges you planned before birth *not* to face in this life. Perhaps you've already cracked them in others, or you've still to attempt them.

The point is that your unshakeable belief in this area of your life simply reinforces any plan you might have made. Rather than just a belief it becomes more like an inner *knowing*. So just imagine what would happen if you could bring the same certainty to other aspects of your life that aren't so favorable?

The other thing that makes your unshakeable belief in any area so empowering is that you *know* it's there so you don't worry about it. One of the hardest aspects of conscious creation is to focus as much as possible while performing creation exercises, but then letting go completely and just allowing the universe to flow and do its thing. Any ongoing worry, or even constant checking for results, will only tighten things up and cause an energetic blockage. So you simply must hang loose, even when it's really hard because your goal is hugely important to you.

Indeed what you should really be aiming for is a sense of nonattachment or detachment exactly as discussed in the previous section. That is, even if your goal is hugely important to you, you'd still be perfectly content if it *didn't* materialize. That's not always easy, but it *is* the best way to guarantee success.

the gap between reality & desire

There's a dichotomy that represents one of the greatest challenges in conscious creation if you're trying to make a major change in your life, such as moving from being poor to rich, for example. On the one hand your words *must* be phrased in the present tense, as in I *am* wealthy, not I *will be* wealthy. But as you already know they must also be absolutely believable to you. So how do you bridge this gap between your current reality and your desired one?

The answer is that you need to believe so much in the changes you've already set in motion that you genuinely do feel and indeed act in the present as if the changes had already taken place. This is the way you change one pattern of engrained behavior for a new one. A really useful tip is that you should take one symbolic action every day to reinforce your belief in your newfound wealth. So even if you have very little money in the present, give just a small amount away to demonstrate that you have more than you need. Or spend just a few pence more on something, maybe a foodstuff that you regularly buy, than you normally would.

From a broader perspective you'll probably have read and heard a great deal about the form of words to use in your affirmations. My advice would be to try not to get too hung up about this, especially if someone tells you to *always* use a specific expression. Play around with what suits you and gets you results, although perhaps take note of common cautions – such as that a *wish* is just a daydream and a *want* is just an admission of lack. Moreover you should focus positively on what you desire, not negatively on what you don't, because creative energies often seem to ignore words like *no* or *not* and just take the main emphasis. Opening phrases such as 'I *am*…', 'I *have…*', 'I *allow…*' and, perhaps best of all, 'I *decide…*' carry huge power of intent.

the gap between beliefs & desires

The reality we all experience is formed by our beliefs, not our desires. If you believe you're lonely, you'll experience that even if surrounded by hundreds of friends. If you believe you're poor, you'll always squander however much money you have to produce the believed rather than desired effect.

So another huge challenge with conscious creation, not always discussed in popular self-help books, is that most of our beliefs about ourselves are hidden away deep in our subconscious. We might consciously desire to manifest the perfect partner, but if deep down we've been conditioned since childhood to have low self esteem, and to feel we're not worthy of true love, we'll keep manifesting far less than perfect partners who'll simply mirror this underlying belief. Until, that is, we unmask and change it.

This is, of course, exactly the dropping of the mask discussed in the previous section. That's why it's so important to complete any necessary work to reveal and transform major unhealthy beliefs that don't serve our desires before we attempt conscious creation in earnest. Otherwise our best efforts may produce only a sense of frustration and failure.

As we saw before, some people may have very little in the way of unhealthy beliefs, so conscious creation may come naturally to them. Others may struggle in one or more areas, and that will tend to suggest there's something that needs to be resolved. In that case, while it's certainly not healthy to *keep* dwelling on problems in the past when you're trying to make a change because repeated focus of that nature only tends to reinforce the unhealthy belief, for some people a degree of focused introspection or even the guidance of a therapist may be required to remove the blockage.

One wonderful piece of advice in this area that's

not commonly discussed is to do the exact opposite of what many manifestation experts tell you. Instead of smothering any doubts you have and pretending they don't exist, listen carefully to what comes up as soon as you give voice to your intention. Don't go actively looking for blockages, then you *would* be putting your focus in the wrong place. Yet specifically when you're in the midst of a creation exercise be a brave spiritual warrior and let your subconscious voice its true concerns and fears, such as 'there's no way I can *really* attract a loving partner, or such a sum of money each month', or whatever it might be. The trick is then to alternate such counter intentions with your positive affirmation of intent.

Focus on one intention and one counter-intention at a time, probably repeating each one no more than three times – five maximum – in any one creation session, although if this can be repeated several times a day so much the better. What you should find is that by continually *facing* the fear it will lose its power over time. This will be especially true if you can become confident enough to actually ridicule it using a silly voice or language, as in 'Oh my God, I am just *soooo* scared that I won't be able to attract a loving partner.' Try it. The fear will soon seem ridiculous and be neutralized.

Incidentally the alternative of endless mantra-like repetition of an intention tends to have little energy and power, because you lose your focus and are just on auto pilot. Less is more.

the layers of the onion

You might be wondering what on earth I can bring to discussion of this treasure when my own attempts at conscious creation over the last two years have been such a conspicuous and continued failure. But the fact is that there was something holding me back all along. I couldn't see it. Those around me couldn't see it. But it was there nonetheless.

For the sake of brevity and simplicity I didn't mention this in my introduction. But only a few weeks before the heartbreak that prompted this book I finally uncovered my major blockage, and that was hugely transformative in its own right. Indeed without taking this step I might not have been strong enough to be ready for THE GIFT when the greatest challenge came.

At the end of a brief but intense relationship with a much younger therapist colleague just about the time my whole life started its downward spiral, she accused me of playing the victim. Given that I was just about to be kicked out of my lovely flat for failing to pay the rent because training work had dropped off, and that she'd just ended our relationship under somewhat strange circumstances, I felt I had every right to feel pretty sorry for myself. Indeed I thought her comments pretty rich coming from someone who'd never had any money worries. That was the first and only time anyone used the v-word as a label for me, and I didn't like it.

Of course I knew I couldn't afford to carry on feeling sorry for myself, and I didn't. I tried lots of different things to turn my life around. I sold my car and bought a plane ticket to Thailand, supposedly to run some workshops at an island retreat for around three months. I was staying a little distance away, and every time I made my way there the woman I needed to see was absent from her office. Nor did the messages I left for her produce any alternative suggestion as to how or when we might get together. After two weeks I felt I had to bail out before I ran out of money completely. The whole thing just felt wrong and left a sour taste.

On my return I organized a series of monthly workshops in London and Dorset, and put a lot of effort into marketing them. But at the end of nine months all twenty-four had had to be cancelled because of insufficient numbers. That was very hard.

Before I moved into my van I tried to see therapy clients when I could, but the number of enquiries was dwindling. I could have put more effort into marketing but the truth was that I'd had a bad run. Virtually every client I'd seen for some time had been challenging, and the experience hadn't been rewarding for them or me. I also had a shocking series of unusual but serious external noise disruptions with difficult clients, which felt more than just a coincidence. Now I don't claim to be the best regression therapist in the world, far from it. But I also know I'm proficient at the very least. So my sense was that this was not where my future lay, at least not for the time being.

After the move to North Dorset I made some more mirrors and other driftwood artwork so I now had a sizeable body of work to sell. These are reasonably elegant and unusual pieces, plus by now I'd made lamps, shelves, clocks and notice boards, so there was plenty of choice. I set up a dedicated website and my sister put a wonderful brochure together and sent it to one of her wealthy contacts, but this produced nothing. Undaunted, the following summer I took a stall at one of the largest country fairs in the UK. Despite a steady stream of visitors to our marquee, as we packed everything up my friends and I couldn't really believe we hadn't managed to sell a single piece.

I guess all these were just diversions, because I've always had a deep sense that my unique gift lies in my writing and research anyway. So I decided to see if I could turn my hand to writing fiction as another way of getting important spiritual messages out to people. I wrote two short novels in a pretty brief space of time because they flowed really well, and I thoroughly enjoyed the different creative process of plots and characters. What's more most people who read through the manuscripts thought they were pretty good. But they steadfastly refused to make any broader impression, and to this day less than fifty copies of each have been sold.

The point of all this is to show that I didn't hide away and give up. I kept plugging away, trying different things, even though it became harder and harder with each new failure. That's why, every time I revisited the victim question I came up with the same answer. No. You're *still* trying really hard, you're just not getting any breaks.

Everyone I knew saw it that way too.

While all this was going on I kept asking my higher self to show me if there was something I was missing, and to help me uncover any blockage that remained. But I always I drew a blank. I didn't even get the sense there *was* still a blockage. I guess this is where our higher self sometimes works in mysterious ways, and perhaps everything needed to unfold exactly as it did in order that I'd have the best possible chance of life-changing transformation.

Nevertheless about nine months ago I *did* have a regression therapy session with a close friend and colleague, with the specific intention of uncovering anything that was holding me back. An interesting past life emerged in which I'd been the ruler of a small desert kingdom, who'd just come to power when he made a huge error of judgment sentencing an innocent man to death. His father had in turn ambushed and killed me. It seems the emotion I carried with me was that I couldn't have power, influence *and* wisdom, and the underlying message was this had been holding back my books. This made sense and felt authentic, so for a while I thought we'd cracked it. But we hadn't.

I also had some fascinating experiences with conscious creation in the run up to uncovering my blockage. For a little while I'd been back in touch with a close friend in London who runs out-of-body workshops and all manner of manifestation jaunts. Indeed our extensive conversations had produced a complete shift in my spiritual worldview and led me to start writing a new book called *Supersoul*, which is still in progress now. This has been like a new lease of life for me, and represents *another* hugely important recent development that probably readied me for THE GIFT.

In any case the friend in question talked me through his manifestation techniques, and I started to put them into practice with what seemed like incredible initial results. Every time I meditated and instructed myself to go to 'the plane of creation' my body would almost go into spasm, and it was quite clear something was going on at an energetic level. This had been happening for several years but not with *this* intensity. My most pressing requirement was money, not least because my car had just blown a head gasket. Within literally five minutes of my first manifestation session a call came through about a day's training work the following week. The money would be just enough to fix the car.

Within three hours of the second session about a week later, an email came through enquiring about my availability for five days work in India. What's more within four hours of the third session a similar enquiry about eight days work in Macedonia. For some time I'd hardly received any offers of training work at all, so quite clearly *something* was happening. But neither of these other offers of work came to fruition and the enquiries dried up again, even though I carried on with the manifestation sessions.

Then, after a gap of nearly two months, the blockage finally revealed itself. By now I was hard at work on *Supersoul* and on this particular day I'd spent about four hours at my desk in intense concentration. It was now six o'clock and I checked my emails – and there was a request to do five days training in London the following week. But it had been sent three hours before, and I wouldn't have been the only person it was sent to.

My heart was racing as I replied. My financial situation was now so precarious that the prospect of stacking supermarket shelves was looming large. Now all I could do was wait. Even after the recent false starts I felt sure the universe wouldn't take a rise out of me again, especially since only once in five years had I ever lost work by not responding quickly enough. This was clearly confirmed work rather than just an enquiry and I was convinced it would come through.

Which is why it was like a knife through the heart when the email arrived later that night offering profuse apologies but the work had already been allocated to someone else. I was in a daze. Yet even as I absorbed this terrible news a little inner voice was saying: 'It's ok. You don't have to succumb to this. There will be something else.' But it was so faint I could hardly hear it, and so much in contrast to my real-life experience for months now I *chose* not to listen to it.

Even as I lay in bed that night, tears streaming and trying to stave off the panic attacks yet again, the voice was there. But so, so quiet. Again I *chose* to ignore it.

When the email came through the following day from a different company asking me to do three days work in December, it all finally fell into place. I must reemphasize at this point that there's no coincidence about all this. The work enquiries I've discussed here are not ones I've selected from a whole load more in order to conveniently illustrate my point. They represent *all* the enquiries I've had in the last six months, and their timing is quite startling.

The little voice had of course been right. I didn't *have* to fall into despair. I didn't *have* to lose all hope, even temporarily. Yes of course it was easy to understand why I did after everything I'd been through. But I still had a *choice*... and just as I had on numerous occasions over the last two years, that night I'd *chosen* to go into *victim* mode. The truth was out at last.

Don't get me wrong. What I've faced over these last few years hasn't been an illusion, and I haven't exaggerated the level of the challenges. But every time I had a choice to either see them as such and determine to overcome them by hook or by crook, or to take the self indulgent way out of curling up in bed and wallowing in victimhood. Making this latter choice, even if only for an hour or day or two at a time, had been having a hugely detrimental effect on my life. Indeed each bout of victimhood had simply manifested another opportunity for me to be just that, whatever other more-positive efforts I might have made in between.

What's even more interesting is that in my early teens at boarding school I'd been mercilessly bullied for two years. So I had a ready-made victim archetype to tap into – even though this wasn't coming through on a conscious level at all, so that it's only now I can see how it all fits together.

What can we take from all this? I guess the lesson is that if life is a struggle in any area for any significant length of time it almost certainly means there's something we need to uncover and transform. What's more we may need to be incredibly tenacious to root it out.

Nevertheless I sincerely hope my somewhat extreme experience represents the exception rather than the rule.

conscious creation versus life plans

So let's return to that most interesting of questions. Did I set all this up as part of my life plan so I could learn about various aspects of self transformation under the most trying of circumstances – and then share that with you? Possibly. In which case you'd have to argue that maybe it pretty much all had to go the way it did.

But it's also perfectly possible that only normal manifestation processes were at work. Every time I went into victim mode and spent any time putting such thoughts out there, I was simply setting myself up for more of the same.

Indeed look at the partner I manifested for myself. When we first fell for each other I was much stronger and she was more blasé, so for about the first six months we'd speak on the phone every night and text all day long. But as her problems at home intensified as reality set in she morphed into the perfect victim's partner. She would repeatedly push me away or just ignore me for days on end, often trying to pretend I didn't even exist as she battled with her guilt about her children. What's more I allowed that to continue, partly because I was learning a huge amount about my own capacity to love, but also because by now I'd grown progressively weaker and it's what victims do.

In reality I'm pretty sure that life planning and normal manifestation processes have combined to create my experience over these last few years. Indeed the two weren't even at odds with each other. I had a life plan that included a victim personality who needed to be exposed and eradicated once and for all, and that very element within me subconsciously manifested the events I experienced during this final showdown.

Indeed that's very likely how it is for most people most of the time. The very emotional shortcomings we bring into incarnation to work on subconsciously manifest exactly the sort of experiences we need unless or until we transform them. So there's no tension between the manifestation dynamic and the life plan.

Where tension does creep in, of course, is when there's a gap between the conscious *desire* and the life plan. I'd expect souls who still have significant challenges to meet as part of their growth to struggle with some or even most aspects of conscious creation until their underlying emotional blockages have been dealt with. In these situations it's probably best to stop trying to struggle *against* the flow and just surrender to it while you sort out your 'stuff'. After all, the flow itself is almost certainly that of your soul and its plan for this life.

Yet there's a rider to this that I feel I can state with some certainty. Ultimately it's *always* an option to take the conscious decision to completely release yourself from all constraints and blockages that might hamper your ability to have a fully abundant life – whatever they might be and whatever lives they might have arisen in. In other words you can *choose* to wipe the slate clean in an instant, without going back and healing or transforming anything. You can *choose* to put yourself into a state of grace just by using the power of total belief.

I don't think we should kid ourselves that this option will be easily put into effect by anyone and everyone. But I *do* think it's possible that increasing numbers of more experienced souls have been receiving what we might call 'injections of grace' from nonphysical sources as part of the global shift in consciousness that's been progressing for some decades now.

Yet my own view — and not everyone will agree with this — is that there are no free gifts when you're transforming your consciousness. If I'm right, even this speeding up of the transformation process would only be gifted because the recipients had previously put the hard yards in. What's more I suspect they'd still have to consistently apply themselves to making the three treasures an integral part of their very being, because any complacency could easily slide them back into old, less favorable patterns of behavior.

the power of past & probable selves

Another way to reinforce your belief in your ability to fundamentally change your life in one or more key areas is to appreciate the power of past and probable selves.

In my own case, once my victim personality had been fully revealed in all his glory I made a solemn pledge to myself that he would *never* be allowed to emerge again, *come what may*. No transformation of current or past life hurts was required. The simple realization of the impact he'd been having on my life was enough for me to banish him for ever. Even as I wrote in my diary that I'd never allow myself to play the victim ever again, it was one of those deep inner knowings I spoke of earlier. Of course it wasn't long before it was fully tested by the final heartbreak and came through with flying colors.

Victim eliminated, who did I want to be instead? I know I'm jumping ahead a little but, just *after* the final heartbreak while I was forcing myself to crack on with research for *Supersoul*, I found myself becoming reacquainted with the work of that most wonderful source of channeled wisdom, Jane Roberts' *Seth*. It was again no coincidence that my attention was caught by some hugely valuable practical material that was not for the new book but would help me with my own transformation right at that moment.

He was talking about how each of us has other

'probable selves' that exist in other realities. This isn't the place to get into exactly what he means, but at the time the very thought that there were other versions of me who *were* loved, successful, popular and wealthy, and who I could *choose* to bring into this reality *at any time*, had real resonance and power. I hope it may have for you too, either now or at some point in the future.

The focus date for the global transformation, 21 12 2012, was now only two days off. Although I was pretty sure this was a purely symbolic date that had no underlying significance apart from what we ourselves had imbued it with, it still seemed to be an excellent opportunity to bring these other selves into play. So I and my two closest friends set out for my favorite sacred space of all, high up on the Purbeck Ridge.

Except when I went into deep meditation and the familiar spasms started, that's not what I did at all. Don't forget your higher self always knows best, and it woke me up to the realization that I didn't need to reach *out* to *other* realities and probable selves to transform my life now. I merely had to reach *within* to other aspects of myself who'd been dominant at earlier times in my *current* life.

Of course there's nothing unusual about this. Basic hypnotherapy works by getting the client to reach back into the past to a time when they *were* confident or slim or whatever it is they want to be again, and anchoring that as something they can bring into their life now. What's more, when used properly past-life therapy can involve deliberately seeking out past lives where strengths that are now missing can be tapped back into.

Yet as I lay there feeling the power of these old me's flooding back in – the popular, deeply-loved me, the successful and widely respected me, the wealthy, money-no-object me – it was hugely transformative and totally unexpected. The best experiences always are. Of course I'm bringing them back into play with a difference. The old me's combined to produce a man who was selfish, materialistic, insensitive and didn't know how to love himself, let alone anyone else. The new one has spirituality and love as his very core.

So if you want to affect a similar transformation, you may not have to reach out to other probable or even past-life selves. If they're there, it's much easier to tap back into other aspects of your current self you know all too well, who've simply lain dormant for too long.

Except, as I said before, I hope most of you won't have comprehensively lost touch with quite so many of them as I did.

To close this section, it's probably true that desires based on kindness and love for yourself and others have a much better chance of being fulfilled than those that are fear-based. Similarly if they're based on cooperation rather than competition – you certainly shouldn't be attempting to influence someone else in any sort of way that might be detrimental to them.

Nevertheless to be realistic we should recognize that conscious creation can at least theoretically be used for *anything*, especially if the belief is strong enough. It doesn't *have* to be altruistic, and it doesn't *have* to involve love.

This is where the third treasure comes into play.

the treasure of

being
love

The spiritual warrior understands that the battle they're involved in isn't one of good against evil, because these are merely human constructs that obscure rather than magnify truth. Rather it centers on the struggle of our dualistic, angst-ridden *human* nature against our true, loving, *soul* nature. This latter aspect finds it easy to just *be* love. Unconditionally, universally, absolutely, totally, in every situation, with everyone, at all times. The trick is to tap into it when we're *most* in pain, and have nothing to gain but the retention of our inner peace.

As always there are a number of aspects to this treasure and THE GIFT, being the most challenging of all, will be left til last.

selfless giving

We all know people who seem tireless in their pursuit of the happiness of others. I'm not talking about those who do it to make themselves feel better, or look better, or just to avoid facing up to things in their own life. Such people might actually do some good, which is terrific, but from the perspective of their own journey they're not coming from the heart, and from genuine, unconditional love.

Instead I'm talking about people for whom nothing seems to be too much trouble. Who volunteer for everything with a big smile on their face. Whose own problems are always regarded as completely insignificant compared to those of others. Who are always there with a helping hand, a shoulder to cry on and to lend an ear. Yet who would never dream of asking for or even needing any of these in return.

I know at least one such person. He's my best friend. As is the way he's spent most of his life only dimly aware of the word *spiritual*, let alone understanding that it applies to him so much more than many who do use it. His very existence, and the example he sets, are a source of unbounded joy to me.

choosing love over fear

It's common enough knowledge now that all emotions stem from one of only two prime sources: love or fear. The spiritual warrior always does everything in their power to react to any situation with the former not the latter. Any fear-based reaction literally produces a dis-ease in the body, at first energetically, but if it's allowed to continue it may well become fully physical. A love-based one just reinforces inner peace.

But let's make sure we eliminate one of the most widespread misconceptions about the treasure of being love. It does *not* involve pretending everything is perfect when it obviously isn't, and glossing over things that need to be faced. The spiritual warrior doesn't deny genuine emotions that are deserving of expression, but handles them in a healthy way.

We'll find out what this means in due course. But first we have to decide whether the fear-based emotions that arise in any given situation are genuine enough to merit closer attention, or are simply caused by a misguided and non-loving view of it. This is all part of being conscious and vigilant *in the now*.

Probably the easiest check is to ensure you're not making unwarranted *assumptions* or taking things more *personally* than you should. Unless you're an experienced spiritual warrior, all too often you will be. So look behind the obvious in others and *never* judge a stranger, because you *never* have enough information.

Being love generally involves *empathizing* with others and their plight, not because you know them or like them, but unconditionally, even with complete strangers. So the next piece of advice is that you should always make every effort to put yourself in the other person's shoes before you react to a situation. Simply ask yourself, 'what are *they* feeling right now?'

Very often these situations will be completely trivial, but they do happen nonetheless and if you learn to crack *them* then the harder ones can follow. My own example is that it used to drive me crazy when pairs of women at my normally quiet swimming club would insist on talking loudly all the way up and down every tediously slow length. The problem wasn't there when I was swimming myself and had my head mostly underwater, it only emerged when I was relaxing in the sauna.

I really used to let this get to me until a friend gave me the advice I'm passing on now. I then realized they were probably terribly overworked at home, looking after demanding children and husbands and so on, and this was one of their few chances to escape and enjoy themselves all week. Love applied, joy shared, frustration eliminated.

Road rage is another example. Especially as a man confronted by another man, it's *so* easy to drop the guard and respond in kind when someone flicks you the finger or whatever it might be. But I guarantee that if you manage to pause and this time *make up* a little story – his mum has just died, for example, and he's just not coping – then you'll find it easy to at least remain emotionless.

You might even manage a smile and a shrug —
although who knows what would happen to your
sense of self if you took a real risk and offered an
apology when it wasn't even your fault?

The better you get at this the more your sense of
inner peace simply rebels when you try anything
other than a loving reaction.

In another situation where you know much more
about the other person, the empathy route may
not work so well. You may feel you have genuine
and justifiable feelings of say anger, jealousy or
resentment. In such a case it's crucial to recognize
that if something is really upsetting your
equilibrium it *must* be a reaction to something
that needs work in *yourself*. Otherwise you'd find
it easy to just walk away and let go.

It's as simple as that. So be wary of immersing
yourself in self-righteous crusades to right wrongs,
because only very rarely will these have any real
justification. The rest of the time they'll simply be
excuses for not facing the real issue within *you*.
Often its origin can be traced right back to an all-

too-common sense of powerlessness. So you have to try and find a way to take back your power. If the problem is bad enough and persistent enough, and your best efforts seem to be achieving nothing, don't suffer. Be brave and leave, whether it's a person or a job.

Another important part of the toolkit for being love is of course *forgiveness*. It's clearly a loving response that replaces, even nullifies, the typical reactions of anger, jealousy and revenge – even guilt, for which *self*-forgiveness is the antidote. But be clear that you can forgive someone *without* condoning what they did or even wanting to share any time or contact with them again. The important thing here is that the poison of fear is removed.

Again there are various techniques for achieving forgiveness that have been written about at length. One familiar one is to empathize in the way we just discussed, by telling yourself the other person's story from their perspective, even if you're making it up because they can't or won't talk to you any more. Another is to actively wish the person you perceive to have wronged you well, because the more you do this the more it will melt your pain until it no longer exists. As it turns out this was the first technique I used when I was discovering THE GIFT, as we'll see in due course, except that for me no element of forgiveness was involved.

An even more *radical* forgiveness technique is to assume everything that happens in your life has been manifested *by* you for a reason, and it's always the perfect experience for your own spiritual growth. Using this technique you're encouraged to ignore the whys and wherefores and just believe that what happened is perfect for you, as long as you let your anger go. Apparently this really works for lots of people, which is great.

As we'll also see shortly, in one sense this is exactly how I've come to view my own situation: as having all been perfect for the achievement of the goal. The difference is that for me there's still been a lot of effort to understand what the goal is and the dynamics underlying everything that has happened. What's more I have a strong feeling that the spiritual warrior will see that as an essential part of the transformation.

THE GIFT: the sword of love

Just as with the treasure of inner peace, you can only really tell if you've mastered the treasure of being love when it's tested under the hardest of circumstances.

So this most challenging aspect of the treasure, THE GIFT itself, forces you to enter mostly uncharted territory by taking up the sword of love to cut your worst fears off at source *as they arise*. It requires enormous courage. But if you're ready to use it, you'll truly prove to yourself that while pain is inevitable suffering is a choice. I know from personal experience this is the prize that awaits you.

What we're talking about here is more than selflessness, empathy or forgiveness, and especially more than *choosing* to react with love rather than fear, as important as all these are. THE GIFT actively *turns* our *worst* fears *into* love. Both approaches should instantly rob fear of any future power, and the distinction is a subtle one. But in my view it's an important one too. I guess in one sense it's also about 'degree of difficulty'.

So if you feel you can *choose* the love rather than fear-based response just by looking at a situation through different eyes, for example, and you don't have to *face* the fear as such, then THE GIFT almost certainly doesn't apply. You only start to enter its territory when one of your *worst* fears is suddenly so alive and active that it's threatening to engulf you in the moment. We're now talking about a fear that's very real and in a sense 'justifiable'.

You could of course try to run away from it, or you could just give in and let yourself drown in it for however long you choose. But you do have another option. You can become the ultimate spiritual warrior, the ultimate alchemist. You can take the fear on and look it right in the eyes as you thrust your sword in, holding on tight and firm as it *transmutes* into love. This, then, is THE GIFT. If my description sounds richly poetic but a little over the top, please believe that it's as close as I can come to describing what actually happened to me.

What do I mean by *worst* fears? Only each of us can decide that for ourselves, which is why there can be no hard and fast rules about when THE GIFT might come into play. I only know about it from the perspective of heartbreak, and in particular 'losing' my love to someone else. We'll come to my personal experience in due course, but in the meantime anything I'm about to say about the other situations in which it *might* play a part is pure conjecture and should be treated as such.

Most of you will have heard of the 'five stages of grief'. They are denial, anger, bargaining, depression and acceptance, and if someone is determined to go through each of these in full it *can* take an age, literally years, for them to get to the point of acceptance. Even then there probably won't be any real 'closure', just an emotional reaction so dulled by repetition that it no longer has much effect. This is the pain of grief feeding through into suffering at its worst.

These are intended to cover any sort of catastrophic personal loss falling under any of the six aspects of life, including things like losing your job or a partner calling time on a failing relationship. But with these latter we tend to be quite clear that if grief is appropriate at all it should only have a limited time span before we should get a grip, bounce back, see it as a new opportunity, get back on the horse, plenty more fish in the sea and so on and so forth.

If we now turn to loss by bereavement – of a friend or family member, a partner or spouse, even a child – we enter those realms where grief is regarded as totally acceptable and even necessary. I'm not trying to overturn millennia of basic psychology by suggesting it's not, for *most* people *most* of the time. But there are limits, and they're clearly exposed if we examine what's feeding the grief. As long as it remains primarily driven by respect and *love* for the departed it will be healthy. But if it ever morphs into a morbid *fear* of not being able to cope with the loss it becomes selfish and unhealthy.

Our advice for most fears is to face them down, isn't it? So isn't that what we should do with grief once it crosses the line? The problem is of course that even the closest friends and best therapists will understandably shy away from intruding on someone's grief and daring to suggest 'time's up'.

Any sort of bereavement is hard, but if there's any element of surprise or the person is taken before their time it's especially so. I've lost both my parents, my father in his eighties, my mother when she wasn't quite seventy, and the latter was harder. This had nothing to do with the level of love I had, which happened to be very high for both of them, but because it was bordering on being 'before her time' and was also more sudden.

My youngest sister was killed in a car accident when only in her thirties, which was far worse still. I loved her dearly too, she was a child of the earth and the type of selfless giver I talked about earlier. Yet for all that I've always openly admitted that the pain of each of these three bereavements added together doesn't get close to the heartbreak of one lost love. For me at least the connection with a partner is a totally different one, with a totally different quality and intensity, and I suspect most people feel that way too.

I suspect therefore that the only loss that can rival heartbreak, indeed quite probably outpaces it by some distance in terms of pain, is that of one's own child. I can't speak about this from personal experience, but I can well imagine that to talk about this as a gift rather than a challenge would be seen as nigh on impossible. The closest the bereaved parent can come is surely to see the *life* of their child as a gift, but not their *loss*.

Even if they're taken by ill-health or other natural cause, the obvious reaction is still: 'Why me?'

'Why us?' It goes hard against the grain when a parent outlives a child. So at best there may be a tendency towards confusion and self pity, at worst downright anger – probably directed at God unless the person is a committed atheist. The reaction will also depend on how sudden the loss was, and whether there was any time to prepare.

Yet we've all witnessed the inspirational courage of those who've lost a child through illness who spend the rest of their lives raising funds to find a cure. This *is* love conquering fear. This *is* hope conquering despair.

But it *isn't*, as far as I can judge, THE GIFT in action. For that I think one of the distinguishing features will normally be that someone else is involved. So we need to bring in an element of accident such as a car crash, or worse still deliberate murder. Here the potential for anger will be magnified hugely because it has a *target* to latch onto. This I think is when THE GIFT can start to come into play.

In the worst cases we've watched parents

tortured by their loss campaigning for the stiffest sentences possible for the 'evil scum' who murdered their child. No one can fail to *understand* their reaction, but nor can we escape the conclusion that their pain is almost certainly consuming them from the inside, and will continue to do so until it's properly faced.

So let's peg it back a little and consider the case of a child killed in a car accident where the driver wasn't breaking the law in any way – let's say they simply hit a patch of black ice. Forgiveness seems much easier now, doesn't it? It doesn't even seem beyond all possibility that the parent might hope the driver finds some peace of mind and can forgive themselves – or that they might even try to help them do this by writing or visiting. What if they even went as far as talking through the driver's experience of the accident and subsequent feelings of horror, and bombarded them with love the whole time?

Now I think we're into proper GIFT territory, because this wonderful, courageous, loving parent is doing some seriously active transmutation.

So can you imagine that same courageous parent acting in the same way with a driver who was speeding, or on their mobile phone?

It would be harder again. That's exactly why I suspect it would be THE GIFT at its glorious best.

a past-life connection

I've been regressed into a number of past lives over the years, and as with most people they form a complete mixture. Several were very ordinary. The First World War soldier who enjoyed the thrill of the wind in his hair as he rode his motorbike down tree-lined, sun-dappled lanes before being killed in the trenches. The drunken young farmer falling off tables before being hanged for a murder he didn't commit. The pregnant native girl on a Pacific island anxiously awaiting a husband who never returned from a fishing expedition.

Several involved Europe and the Inquisition. The member of the establishment who rebelled and was tortured to death for his pains, fingernails removed one by one. The itinerant preacher who gained so much support that instead of the luxury of torture and death they preferred to lock me away, shackled to a chair and wearing an iron helmet so heavy I could never properly sleep.

Several involved a different spiritual calling. The terrified young Mediterranean boy just about to have his eyes burned out for possessing 'second sight', who then helped people as a hermit and lived into old age. The young man preaching a message of pure love to a crowd of thousands in the Near East in the generation immediately after Jesus. I sense this latter is authentic because of the meandering way I was taken there via another life, otherwise I'd simply have rejected it as ego. But as my colleague wisely pointed out as I lay there stunned by the power of reliving the scene: 'We've all been teachers at one time.'

None of these ever involved the sort of conventional, unresolved issues that needed healing and reframing. Whenever I was asked how

I felt after death the reply was always a breezy, 'No worries, we all knew the parts we were playing and what we had to do.' In truth that feels as genuine now as it did then. I don't think any of these lives *did* need healing.

What about lives that at least have a relevance to my current one? I strongly suspect that the Near Eastern preacher and the two men involved with the Inquisition were intended to act as sources of courage and inspiration for the path I've chosen in this life. Meanwhile the desert ruler I described in the last section was deliberately sought as a possible source of current problems.

Yet there is one life I haven't mentioned. As it turns out it was one of the earliest I experienced, emerging on the first module of my regression training. I was a dark, brooding little boy in a small country school, sat next to his more sociable brother. I was hit by an energetic bolt of lightning as a new little girl walked into the class. Never has love been so immediate and all-consuming, despite my tender years.

The three of us became constant companions. She loved us both dearly. But when the time came she chose him. Just before their wedding she and I rode out alone for a picnic and I was so close to saying all the things I'd kept to myself, but I stayed silent out of love for my brother. At the ceremony I sat alone in a corner getting drunk as the whole village celebrated. From that moment on I hardly moved from my home, and the rocking chair that looked out across the fields. I lived that lonely, reclusive life for nearly four more decades before my broken heart finally killed me.

At the time we received the message that I had to learn to be comfortable in my own skin, with no partner, and still be happy for others who are in love rather than jealous of them. Before things started to spiral downhill for me I felt I'd taken that on board and this time was passing the test.

Apart from building it into one of my novels, that life didn't come back to me at all until I started to write this last and most crucial part of the book. Suddenly I realized that hadn't been the end of it at all. As soon as my love in this life transferred her affections to someone else I was once again facing virtually the same challenges: of being happy not for lovers generally, but for her *in particular*; and of not falling into a mire of self pity and despair. Finally it all made sense. I felt genuine pride that a challenge that had tortured and eventually killed me in one life was now allowing me to make perhaps the most fundamental and important transformation of all in this.

discovering THE GIFT

To pick up from where we left off in the first section, when her husband moved back in we agreed to have no contact, and that lasted probably for about a month before the texts started again, and then a brief flurry of meetings for one reason or another that were still wonderful and sensual, even if we were attempting to downplay the sexual side of things. Not only that but we proved yet again that whatever stresses and strains we faced melted away when we were actually face to face, and could talk to each other properly and with love and compassion.

We both felt we'd reached a point of serenity that could only be ruffled if and when I met someone else, a possibility we'd of course had to openly discuss as soon as she decided to resume her marriage. But the talk was of allowing ourselves more regular time together, even though it could never be much, while we waited to see what would unfold.

Then, almost immediately, she was off again, becoming increasingly distant from a personal perspective – even though on a professional level she'd kindly agreed to provide me with invaluable feedback on the early chapters of *Supersoul*. She was becoming increasingly busy with her own work, but I knew in my bones that wasn't the totality of it and I wasn't happy. This kind of about turn had just happened way too many times. So two weeks before Christmas I phoned her and told her that now I was no longer a victim I valued myself way too much to be messed about.

She was quiet, but when pushed said she felt she had to concentrate on her family, as well as that I needed to be completely free to meet someone else. So friends only. It wasn't a reversal I expected or wanted, but because I loved her I agreed to do as she asked. Did she still love me? She said yes, and it felt real. Why wouldn't it? She'd maintained for a long time that she would probably always love me. That's how special our love felt. To both of us.

I sent a couple of cursory texts over the next week, saddened at the prospect of another Christmas without her. They were honest and loving but I wasn't trying to change anything.

Then, exactly a week later, d-day arrived.

It was mid morning when the text came through. It was her, saying she knew absolutely and without any possible doubt whatsoever that we would only ever be able to be friends from now on, nothing more. In truth to start with I was more bemused than anything, because I'd had at least two of these since I met her. But not recently, and not when we'd been placing such a premium on staying open to whatever might come.

Given that her last words to me one week before had been that her feelings were still the same, it became pretty clear that something must have happened to make her shut me down so harshly and out of the blue. But I was still calm as I called her. No answer. This was pretty typical too unfortunately, she did have a habit of dropping bombshells by text and then not making time to talk to me properly. When four or five attempts to call were ignored it looked very much as if it was going to be the same all over again.

Then a quick text saying she was busy all day and couldn't talk. Thanks a lot! I asked what was going on, she said nothing, then when pressed she admitted that 'something' had happened. All of a sudden it hit me that, against all the odds, when it should have been me or her husband meeting someone new, it must have happened to *her*. But at first I could scarce believe it. I asked her outright, and the wait began. It was torture.

Around four hours later I received a text explaining what was going on: 'His name is… He lives abroad and I met him one week ago on a healing course. As soon as I started working on him there was an incredible energetic connection. I was glad he was flying home afterwards, and tried to avoid him but he cancelled his flight. We've shared at least one life, as twins. He even answers questions that are in my head before I've said them.'

Anyone who's had their heart broken will understand exactly what I was feeling at that point. Anyone who hasn't will struggle, whatever words I tried to use.

To make matters worse, probably my deepest love before this was with the girl who first introduced me to spiritual matters a long, long time ago. She too had met someone else almost immediately we broke up, and I got a strong sense they had a telepathic bond. It had made me really jealous. So this situation now had pretty much everything I needed to be totally and utterly triggered.

All that evening I managed to distract myself talking to and texting mutual friends. None of them could believe it either, they'd all heard her talking about me and knew how we both felt. Apart from her own best friend who, it turned out, had been putting the new man up. She told me he was good for her – and I wasn't? – and that I should just let her go with love.

During the night I kept chanting 'stay conscious' to myself over and over again to keep the worst of the tears and panic at bay. I even managed to snatch some sleep. At around three in the morning I sent her a very loving text telling her how much I hoped he would give her the strength to complete what her love for me hadn't been able to. Moreover that they, her boys and her husband might all now find some true happiness and peace. My words came from the heart and I was proud of myself as I energetically cut the chords with her for the umpteenth and last time.

But I knew that wasn't the end of it for me. The

next morning I managed a shower and when I got back to the van the bed was looking very enticing. I could just curl up, let the tears flow, shut the world out and welcome my inner victim back with open arms. The pull was *incredibly* strong. But thank god I didn't give in. I might have still been there now, and none of the wonderful things I'm just about to relate would have happened.

I dressed and sat myself down at my desk, acutely aware that I needed to occupy my mind as much as possible. I began some research for *Supersoul* and it was going surprisingly well when I noticed it. My old friend heartache, who hadn't been in my life for a few years now, was back with a vengeance. You all know the dull ache in your chest, the dis-ease that's always there in the background, whatever you're doing. He's here at least for Christmas and New Year, I thought. I can consciously control my thoughts to a significant degree, but I can't control him. Great!

Then something else happened. An inner voice said, quite emphatically: 'Go into it! Go into the feeling and find out what it is.' I focused inwards onto the pain. There was some self pity and loneliness, some simple missing her, but also a big chunk of jealousy over what she'd found with someone else, and all the things they'd now share that we'd planned to. 'Just repeat what you told her last night,' said the voice. So I began to chant, 'I am genuinely *happy* for her.'

For me this was the first part of THE GIFT. I was stunned when almost immediately, possibly after only one or two repetitions, the pain in my chest *simply vanished*. Literally. No trace. I was still worried it might make a comeback at some point, but no. As each day went by I realized *it had gone and was never coming back*. Just one injection of love was enough in this case.

But the really powerful aspect did not come til the following day. She was almost completely ignoring me, which was to be expected even if a little harsh, but a brief text that morning said she'd be busy all day. I had a strong sense the two of them would be spending it together and almost immediately a different pain came, a much sharper one. Again the inner voice was insistent: 'Face it. Don't run away, go right into it.'

This was a different proposition altogether. I was very uneasy, and for a while I sat and pondered what to do while the pain lurked. Then I took up the sword of love, although I didn't know that's what I was doing at the time – indeed I had no idea what was going to happen. 'What's one of the most painful things you can imagine?' prompted the voice, and immediately I found myself in a scene where she was gently caressing his cheek and telling him how much she loved him. The tears started to flow and I began to shake.

'Push on through Ian. You *can* do this!' I focused more and more intently on them and, suddenly, I broke through the pain barrier. That's exactly what it felt like as I relaxed into *their* joy at having found each other. Now we were all one, their joy was my joy, and there was no need to make distinctions any more. My tears of pain, jealousy and fear had morphed into tears of joy and love.

I barely paused for breath as I knew what I must do next. I had to go the whole way, into the worst pain of all, right here, right now while my sword was drawn. I began to imagine them making love to each other, slowly and tenderly. This was much, much harder. I was deliberately putting in some detail to force me to stick with it and the sobbing and shaking were much more violent than before. At one point it became almost unbearable, but I hung on tight.

Then there it was again. Barrier smashed down. Their love was my love, their joy was my joy, their ecstasy was my ecstasy. The essence of my tears had changed once again as fear and pain had been transmuted into love.

It didn't matter whether what I imagined had already happened, was happening as I imagined it, or only would happen at some point in the future. I was pretty sure this was a hugely powerful and transformative experience rather than just a rather sick mindgame.

Any doubts were completely expelled when I went for a walk a little later. I saw a young couple strolling arm in arm and burst into tears — not through jealousy but because I was simply sharing their joy. I phoned a close friend that night and his response was, 'Wow! If it's all exactly as you say, that's *Buddha* like!'

Two days later I was discussing it with my two closest friends when the idea for this book started to emerge.

the proof of the pudding

Since that time it's increasingly seemed to me that all this has really been a masterly plan to help me take a major step forwards in changing my consciousness. So many things had to come together for it to work.

I had to reach rock bottom and lose everything so I could finally identify and eliminate my victim archetype. I had to find the strength of the new lease of life my research for *Supersoul* has given me. But I also had to love her enough that when the big moment came the heartbreak was still all too real. Meanwhile she had to fall for someone else not because we had a problem so she was 'ready' and 'looking', but purely and simply because she was suddenly confronted by a bond even more special than ours. That way I'd have no alternative but to accept the situation and wish her well, rather than get angry or try to fight it.

If any one of these ingredients had been missing THE GIFT could easily have passed me by. The fact that they all combined together in the run up to 21 12 2012 may or may not give them added significance. As may the fact that this book has emerged out of it all too.

As I write it's been nearly three weeks since the bombshell struck. On reflection I could quite understand some of you thinking my heartbreak experience is relatively trivial in comparison to some of the bereavement challenges I discussed above. Especially when we hardly ever saw each other, weren't married, didn't have children with each other and so on. You may well be right. But still I know when heartbreak is very real, and this was. What's more those you who've suffered it too, which is probably most of you, will know that to defeat it this quickly and this comprehensively is something quite special.

I've just got through the whole festive period without a single moment's genuine suffering. That's not because I tried to turn my attention to someone else in an ultimately fruitless attempt to avoid any pain, or because I was involved in some massive social extravaganza. I was with family over Christmas, then for four days spanning the New Year I was laid up in bed alone in my van, which is extremely rare for me. I was so ill I had to suspend work on this book, and was hugely grateful when the constant headache and nightly insomnia and delirium left me and I could just eat and be human again.

Still no return of the victim.

More important again, still no *suffering*. Not even mixed emotions when she told me she'd told her boys what was going on, and this time knew she had the strength to make it work for all of them. Just a shared sense of joy.

Don't get me wrong. The *pain* still makes an effort every now and then, and every time it starts to creep in you'll feel the onset of the dis-ease, even if it's duller than at first. It's an old reaction and belief system trying to make a comeback. But you'll find that if you stay observant you'll catch it almost before it starts, and that may well be enough. If it decides to make a more determined effort, as soon as you take the conscious decision to *bombard* it with love it will evaporate.

It simply can't survive in the face of love. It's like a fire without oxygen. A fish out of water.

So I can tell you this right from the heart.

THE GIFT is real...

and it works.

I decided early on that I'd write this book in my own words, even though in many places I could have quoted others who've inspired me. In particular this includes the Pathwork 'guide', whose lectures were channeled by Eva Pierrakos from the 1950s to the 1970s; Seth, the wonderfully wise entity channeled by Jane Roberts in the 1960's and 70s; Neale Donald Walsch's 'God' with whom he conversed so much in the 1990s, whoever or whatever they may have been; Don Miguel Ruiz and his beautifully simple 'Four Agreements'; Eckhart Tolle, whose 'Power of Now' has had such a huge impact on so many; Frederick Dodson, whose wonderfully grounded 'reality creation technique' is certainly the best I've come across; and my great friend Todd Acamesis, with whom I've shared many hours of stimulating conversation on all matters spiritual, who also introduced me to Dodson's work.

In no sense have I done this to ignore or underplay their contribution, but merely to allow my own words to flow, especially when I was also using my own experiences to illustrate the theory.

I've received some wonderful help and encouragement from other close friends too. Ken Huggins came up with the title almost as soon as I mentioned the word 'book' and, in the hour or so discussion that followed, his and his partner Pam's input as a highly qualified hypnotherapist and counselor respectively allowed me to sound out whether THE GIFT really was something a little bit special that I should share with others.

Fellow regression therapists Andrew Perez and Janet Treloar have also been hugely supportive and encouraging. Andrew was the one who referred to THE GIFT as being Buddha-like, and he wisely insisted that I had to write the book as quickly as possible while the events and emotions were fresh in my head. Meanwhile Janet is one of the most gifted therapists I know, and as soon as she heard about it she told me from the heart how very proud she was that I'd been so brave as to confront my worst fears, not knowing what might happen. That meant an awful lot to me.

So all four of them together helped me to

recognize that I could and should write this book. They also took the time to give me constructive feedback on the manuscript, as did two other great pals, Stephen Gawtry and John Straub, the latter rightly insisting that I should attempt to make it accessible to anyone and not just those with experience of the spiritual path.

But of course there's one person I'd like to thank above all others, because without her contribution not only would there have been no book but no chance to experience THE GIFT in the first place. For obvious reasons I've protected her anonymity, even though our close friends know who she is. I simply want to emphasize that, for all its challenges for both of us, our love was very real; and that nothing described in this book should leave anyone with the impression that she is anything other than a wonderful human being.

Indeed they say the people in your life who challenge you most are probably your closest soul mates, because only they would have the love to take on such a demanding job and the determination to see it through. Never have I seen a better example than the one she's provided, and I thank her from the very depths of my being.

As for me, what have been the results of all this self-transformation? In particular, am I now consciously creating the life of full abundance that is everyone's birthright? Well, it's too early to see much in the way of pull-through from the energetic into the physical yet.

But I have this deep inner knowing...

Ian Lawton

7 January 2013

postscript 1

At the beginning of February a number of synchronicities led me to a regression session with John's partner Anita, in order to get to the bottom of a deep sense of suffering and injustice that for the last few years especially has been triggered by certain scenes in films. These included the final torture scene in Braveheart; those leading up to

*the crucifixion in the Passion of Christ; and —
perhaps bizarrely but worst of all — the one near
the beginning of David Lean's version of Dickens'
Oliver where the poor boy is thrown out of the
undertakers through no fault of his own and
forced to tramp his way to London.*

*Despite my own past-life experiences of torture
and isolation, I assumed this was merely an
expression of a growing sense of universal love.
But, as Todd wisely pointed out, anything that
triggers you to the point of deeply sobbing for
minutes on end must have some personal element
that needs to be examined. So after reliving yet
another life of isolation, this time as an Eskimo
whose wife and family had died because he
couldn't find enough food, I felt the need to speak
to a guide.*

*Whether or not it came from anything other than
my own inner wisdom and intuition, the message
was that my pride, even as a soul, had led me to
repeatedly take on lives of great challenge —
usually involving rejection or isolation. My attitude*

was always slightly impatient, a gung-ho one of 'I can handle this, no problem'.

Yes, I had made great strides, both in terms of my own growth and in contributing to that of the group soul – even if sometimes I didn't pass the test first time round. Yet I was also invited to consider that perhaps enough was enough.

Indeed the message that came through loud and clear is perhaps an important one for all of us:

> *Growth doesn't have to be accomplished by suffering...*

postscript 2

It's now mid-March. I don't want to change the energy of my original author's note, but I've been urged by Andrew to add details of what I've been able to consciously manifest since I removed my victim blockage. The three major intentions I've been working on are to regenerate my finances via training work, to expand my circle of spiritual friends and to irresistibly attract a wonderful new love into my life.

As far as the first is concerned I manifested a completely unexpected introduction to a new company before Christmas, when an assessor from our governing body liked my training style and came back from a coffee break having already been kind enough to make the introduction. It took some weeks to sort out the details but, while we're still in the grips of recession, as I write I'm in the middle of two-and-a-half weeks straight work for them, with bookings for a further three weeks in April. That's some turnaround by anyone's standards.

As far as friends are concerned, also before Christmas I set up a new local meetup group called the 'Spiritual Exchange'. It has now attracted nearly fifty members and we've held four fortnightly meetings with good attendance and wonderful, open and warm-hearted discussion. Even better on a more personal level I've made several new friendships through the group that have opened up important new avenues of *spiritual exploration for me, and which I feel sure will be lifelong.*

I haven't yet manifested a wonderful new love, but I've also sensed the timing isn't quite right. I need to be fully back on my own two feet to come together with another person with no sense of neediness or lack on either side. But that moment is close at hand.

What's more I've made a firm intention that, whatever life plan I might or might not have originally had concerning this, I've now changed it. In my sessions on the plane of creation I sense the two of us being drawn together as if by huge, invisible, cosmic magnets, and my body shakes and spasms under the influence of the powerful energies. So I have absolute conviction about my 'cosmic order', and I can once again say with confidence:

> *I have this deep inner knowing...*

further reading

REINCARNATION EVIDENCE, INTERLIFE PLANNING & THE HOLOGRAPHIC SOUL

Fiction

Lawton, Ian, *The Man Who Didn't Die* (Rational Spirituality Press, 2011).

Non-Fiction (simple)

Lawton, Ian, *The Little Book of the Soul* (Rational Spirituality Press, 2007).

Non-Fiction (comprehensive)

Lawton, Ian, *The Big Book of the Soul* (Rational Spirituality Press, 2008) and Supersoul (RS Press, 2013).

MEDITATION, SYNCHRONICITY & MANIFESTATION

This is just a sample of the books I know best or that have helped me the most. There are many others available.

Fiction

Bach, Richard, *Illusions: The Adventures of a Reluctant Messiah* (Mandarin, 1992).

Coelho, Paulo, *The Alchemist* (HarperCollins, 1995).

Lawton, Ian, *The Girl Who Learned to Live* (RS Press, 2012.

Millman, Dan, *Way of the Peaceful Warrior* (H J Kramer, 1984].

Redfield, James, *The Celestine Prophecy* [Bantam, 1994].

Non-Fiction

Acamesis, Todd, *www.journeyoftruth.co.uk*.

Byrne, Rhonda, *The Secret* (Simon & Schuster, 2006).

Cainer, Jonathan, *Cosmic Ordering* (Collins, 2006).

Dodson, Frederick, *The Reality Creation Technique*, Amazon, 2010.

Lawton, Ian, *Your Holographic Soul and how to make it work for you* (RS Press, 2010).

Roberts, Jane, *The Seth Material* (Prentice Hall, 1970), *Seth Speaks* (Bantam, 1974) and *The Nature of Personal Reality* (Prentice Hall, 1974).

Ruiz, Don Miguel, *The Four Agreements* (Amber-Allen Publishing, 1997).

The Pathwork Lectures (for the full set of 258 lectures see www.pathwork.org, or for an introduction see www.ianlawton.com/se6.htm).

Tolle, Eckhart, *The Power of Now* (Hodder & Stoughton, 2005).

Walsch, Neale Donald, *Conversations with God: Books 1-3* (Hodder & Stoughton, 1997-9).

Wattles, Wallace, *The Science of Getting Rich*, Elizabeth Towne Co, 1910.

other books by the author

all from Rational Spirituality Press *www.rspress.org*

POCKET BOOKS

THE LITTLE BOOK OF THE SOUL (2007) uses a story-book style. It contains a selection of the most interesting near-death and past-life cases that support Rational Spirituality, interspersed with simple summaries and analysis.

YOUR HOLOGRAPHIC SOUL (2010) uses a question-and-answer style. It tackles seven key questions to build a Rational Spiritual framework, and then offers ten self-help suggestions for how we can use it to get the most out of our lives.

THE FUTURE OF THE SOUL (2010) contains crucial channeled messages about 2012 and the global shift in consciousness.

[These three are also available in the large format trilogy AN INTRODUCTION TO THE SOUL.]

RESEARCH BOOKS

SUPERSOUL (2013) contains out-of-body and other evidence that each and every one of us is a holographic reflection of a supersoul that has power way beyond our wildest imaginings.

THE BIG BOOK OF THE SOUL (2008) is the main reference book for Rational Spirituality, containing full details of key cases, in-depth analysis of all key topics and full source references.

THE HISTORY OF THE SOUL (2010) reinterprets the most revered ancient texts and traditions from all around the world about a forgotten golden race that became debased and was wiped out in a catastrophe.

THE WISDOM OF THE SOUL (2007) contains the results of a new style of research that attempts to answer a number of key universal questions by regressing ten subjects into the interlife.

SPIRITUAL NOVELS

THE MAN WHO DIDN'T DIE (2011) is a gripping novel about how a successful businessman's life changes after he kills his beloved wife in a car crash, and finds himself paralyzed from the neck down.

THE GIRL WHO LEARNED TO LIVE (2012) is the moving story of a disadvantaged girl's search for love and fulfillment, and the secrets she uncovers along the way.

AUTOBIOGRAPHY OF AN ANGEL (2014) is a fascinating journey through the experiences of an angel or guide, with some startling twists.

MEMOIRS OF A MESSIAH (2014) is an epic account of a highly experienced soul's efforts to help humanity move forwards, spanning tens of thousands of years.

IAN LAWTON was born in 1959. Formerly an accountant, sales exec, business and IT consultant and avid bike and car racer, in his mid-thirties he changed tack completely to become a writer-researcher specializing in ancient history and, more recently, spiritual philosophy.

In his non-fiction *Books of the Soul* series he has developed the ideas of Rational Spirituality and of the holographic soul, while most recently he has introduced the radical concept of the supersoul. Short film clips discussing all these can be found at *www.ianlawton.com* and on YouTube. He has also written a number of spiritual novels, and is a trained current, past and between life regression therapist.